For Richard
August 2

from Anomy —

A very important chapter in guess life —

Stories
Jesus
told

Illustrated by Toni Goffe
Retold by LaVonne Neff

Tyndale House Publishers, Inc.
Wheaton, Illinois

© 1993 Hunt & Thorpe
Illustrations © 1993 by Toni Goffe
All rights reserved

Published in the United States by
Tyndale House Publishers, Inc.
Wheaton, Illinois
Published in Great Britain by
Hunt & Thorpe

ISBN 0-8423-5943-5
Printed in Singapore.

00 99 98 97 96 95 94 93
9 8 7 6 5 4 3 2 1

Contents

The Farmer and His Seed

Matthew 13:1–23; Mark 4:1–20; Luke 8:4–15

A man went out to plant a field. As he walked along, he scattered seeds on the ground.

Some seeds fell on the hard ground beside the path. Birds quickly snatched them away.

Some seeds fell on rocky ground. They sprang up quickly, but they didn't grow deep roots. When the sun shone hot, the young plants withered and died.

Some seeds fell on thorny ground. They started to grow, but the thorns grew even faster and choked the plants.

Some seeds fell on good soil. They grew deep roots and strong, green leaves. When the plants were big and healthy, they produced much fruit.

Jesus said that the seeds are like God's Word. People who hear God's Word are like the different kinds of ground. What kind of ground do you want to be like? How can you be like that kind of ground?

The Lost Sheep

Matthew 18:12-13; Luke 15:1-7

A man had a hundred sheep. Some were big and some were little. Some were black and some were white. Some were fast and some were slow. He loved each one of them.

Every day the man took his sheep to a pasture where they could eat fresh green grass. Every day he took them to a stream where they could drink clear cold water. Every night he counted them to be sure they were all safe.

One night he counted only ninety-nine sheep. The night was cold and stormy. The man was tired and hungry. But one of his sheep was missing.

The man turned around and went back to the pasture and the stream. He looked up cliffs and down canyons. He looked everywhere until he found the lost sheep.

The man called his friends and neighbors. "Let's celebrate," he said. "I have found my lost sheep."

God loves all his people—even when they wander away from him. What does God do when we are far from him?

The Runaway Son

Luke 15:11–32

A man had two sons. The older son was obedient.
The younger son was not.

The younger son took lots of money and left home.

He spent the money foolishly. Soon it all ran out.

The boy got a job feeding pigs. He was so hungry he wanted to eat the pigs' food. "I could get a better job at my father's house," he thought.

The boy returned home. His father ran out to meet him. "I'm a bad son—," the boy began, but his father interrupted.

"Let's have a party!" he said. "My son has come home!"

The older son was angry. "Why don't you give me a party?" he asked. "I have always obeyed you."

"Everything I own will be yours someday," his father replied. "But today, let's celebrate. I thought my son was dead, and he is alive!"

God is happy when his runaway children come home to him. Why was the older brother angry? Was the father fair to both his sons?

The Two Builders
Matthew 7:24-29; Luke 6:47-49

A wise man decided to build a house. "I will build
on solid rock," he said. "It will never move or
crumble."

"The man ordered bricks. He hired workmen. After

many months, his house was finished.

A foolish man also decided to build a house. "I will build on a sandy beach," he said. "It is easy to build on sand."

The man ordered lumber. He hired workmen. In just a few weeks, his house was finished.

The storms came. It rained and rained. The wind howled. The sea swelled up, and giant waves battered the beach.

High above the sea, the rock did not move. The wise man's house stayed snug and safe.

Down on the beach, the sand began to slip and slide. The foolish man's house trembled and tottered. Then, with a crack and a crash, it slid into the sea.

Jesus is like a solid rock. When we obey him, we are safe.
Why did the wise man's house stay safe? Why did the foolish man's house fall down?

The Wedding Feast

Matthew 22:1-10; Luke 14:16-24

A king planned a great feast for his son's wedding. He invited all the great people of the land: princes and merchants, generals and landowners.

The wedding day came. The king sent his servant to call the guests. But when the servant returned, he was alone. The guests had refused to come.

"I must inspect my new land," said one.

"I must try out my new oxen," said another.

"I must spend time with my new bride," said a third.

The king was angry. He told his servant, "Go back

into town and invite the poor, the crippled, the blind, and the lame."

The servant did as the king commanded. He returned with many guests.

"There is room for still more," said the king. "Go out on the open road and invite migrants and tramps and the homeless. My house will be full for my son's wedding feast."

Jesus said the kingdom of heaven is like this king's feast. Who is invited to come to the kingdom of heaven?

The Rich Man and Lazarus

Luke 16:19-31

There was once a rich man who wore silk and ate pheasant every day.

At his gate lay a poor man named Lazarus. Lazarus was sick, but nobody nursed him. He was hungry, but nobody fed him. The rich man paid no attention to him at all.

Lazarus died, and the angels carried him to Abraham's bosom. The rich man also died, but he was taken to a place of torment.

The rich man looked up and saw Abraham and Lazarus. "Father Abraham!" he cried out. "Send Lazarus to dip his finger in water and cool my tongue."

"I cannot send him," said Abraham. "No one can cross from one side to the other."

"Then," said the rich man, "send him to warn my five brothers, so they do not come here too."

"They have Bibles," Abraham replied. "If they don't read the Bible, they won't listen to Lazarus either."

The Bible tells us to treat others as we would want to be treated. Do you know someone you should treat more kindly?

The Pharisee
and the Tax Collector
Luke 18:9-24

Two men went to the temple to pray. One man was a Pharisee; the other, a tax collector.

The Pharisee was a religious leader. He was known for being good. People respected him.

This is how he prayed:

"God, I thank you that I am not like most people. I am not greedy, unfair, or unfaithful. I pay tithes on all I

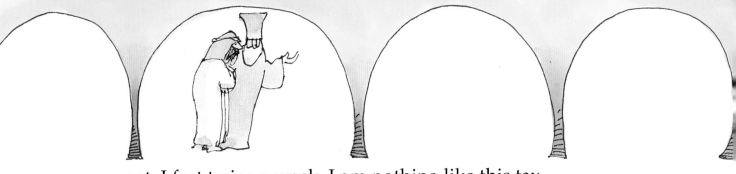

get. I fast twice a week. I am nothing like this tax collector."

The tax collector was a traitor. He was known for cheating. People hated him. He was ashamed of himself, and he stood as far away from the Pharisee as he could.

This is how he prayed: "God, have mercy on me, for I am a sinner."

God forgave the tax collector. He did not forgive the Pharisee.

Jesus said that people who humble themselves will become important, and that people who try to be important will be humbled. Why did God forgive the tax collector? Why did he not forgive the Pharisee?

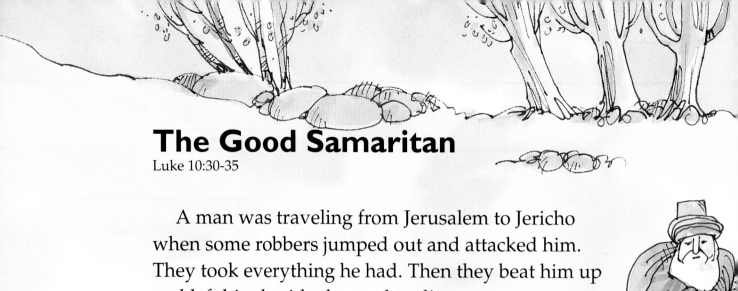

The Good Samaritan

Luke 10:30-35

A man was traveling from Jerusalem to Jericho when some robbers jumped out and attacked him. They took everything he had. Then they beat him up and left him beside the road to die.

A priest came down the road. He saw the dying man. He crossed to the other side of the road and looked the other way.

A Levite came down the road. He saw the dying man. He crossed to the other side of the road and walked quickly by.

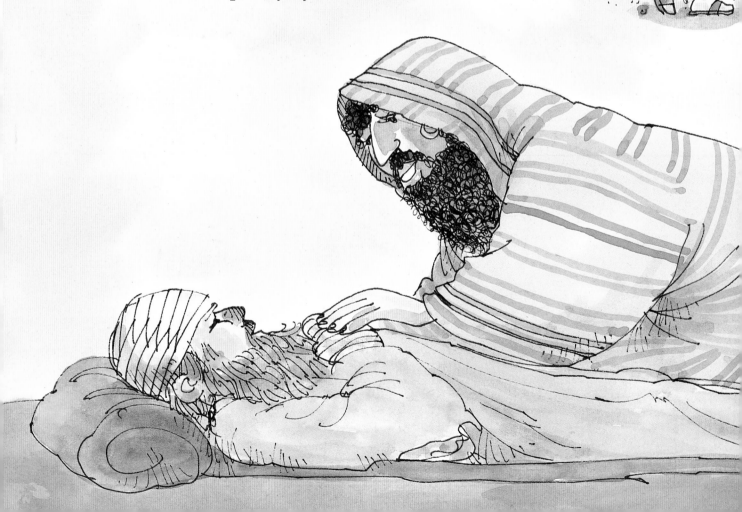

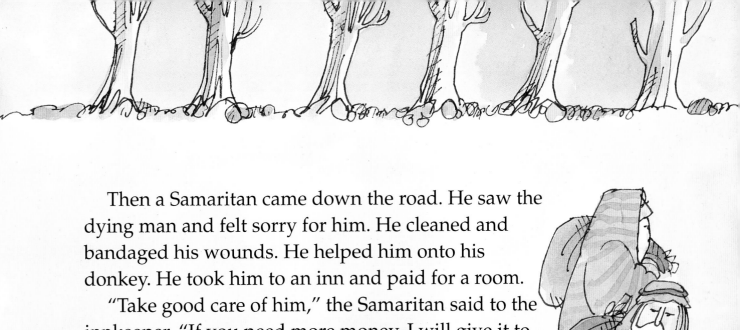

Then a Samaritan came down the road. He saw the dying man and felt sorry for him. He cleaned and bandaged his wounds. He helped him onto his donkey. He took him to an inn and paid for a room.

"Take good care of him," the Samaritan said to the innkeeper. "If you need more money, I will give it to you on my way back."

Samaritans were foreigners. People did not like them. Priests and Levites were religious leaders. People thought they were good. In this story, which man was a good neighbor?

The Workers in the Vineyard

Matthew 20:1-16

Early one morning a man went to the marketplace to find workers for his vineyard. "I will give you one denarius a day," he promised.

At nine o'clock the man returned to the

marketplace and hired more workers. "I will give you a fair wage," he said.

At noon, at three o'clock, and again at five o'clock the man hired still more workers.

When evening came the workers were paid. Those who began work at five o'clock got one denarius each. So did those who began work at three o'clock, at noon, and at nine o'clock.

The workers who had come at daybreak expected more money. They had worked longer than anyone else. But each of them got one denarius.

"This is unfair," they grumbled.

The man said, "Didn't we agree on one denarius? Is it unfair to you if I am generous to the others?"

Jesus told this story to show what the kingdom of heaven is like. Was the man unfair to the first workers? Would you rather be treated fairly or generously? How does God treat you?

The Rich Fool

Luke 12:16–20

Once there was a man who had a very good harvest. He had so much grain that he did not know what to do with it.

He sold some and bought everything he had ever wanted.

He sold some more and piled up bags of money in every room of his house.

And he still had mountains of grain left.

"What shall I do?" he said to himself. "I don't have room for all this."

He thought and he thought. "I know," he finally said. "I will tear down my little barns and build bigger ones. I will put my things and my money and my grain in my new big barns. And then I will retire. I will eat and drink and have a good time."

But God said, "You fool! Tonight you will die, and then who will enjoy your riches?"

Jesus said that money cannot buy a good life. It is better to be rich in God's sight than to have lots of things. What should the rich fool have done with all his grain?